A Journey of Grief, Grace, and Healing

BEYOND THE BREAK

Written by
ANDERAL WARD

With Contributions from
AMBER WARD

Attention: Permissions Coordinator

Welcome To The Storm Publishing!
info@w2tspublishing.net

Ordering Information:
Quantity sales. Special discounts are available on quantity purchases by corporations, associations, and others. For details, contact the publisher at the email address above.

Library of Congress Control Number: 2025922401

ISBN: 978-1-966612-70-4
Cover Design: Kasper Harris of Gifft Grafix
Photo Credit Cover: The Love Gallery, Shola Sogunra

Austin Stephens, Austin S Editing

First Printed Edition: November 2025

Printed in the United States of America

DEDICATION

To Charles Leonard Ward IV (CJ), my forever firstborn—your light did not fade, it multiplied. To my grandson, Cahlil Seph-Ron Marable-Ward—you are the promise fulfilled, and the light entrusted to tomorrow.

To the beloved members of my family who have transitioned. Your presence remains in every prayer, every purpose, every page. Your legacy lives on in the work of my hands and the faith in my heart.

To every mother, sister, daughter, and friend who has lived through loss and chosen to rise again, this is for you. May you find healing, hope, and holy restoration. And to the God who kept me. Thank you for being my anchor in sorrow, my strength in rising, and my light in every dark place.

CONTENTS

ACKNOWLEDGMENTS

First, I want to thank God for giving my co-author and daughter, Amber Bre'naee Ward, and me the courage to share our journey toward healing after the death of my beloved son—her first friend and brother—by suicide. Not in a million years did I imagine I would join the ranks of mothers who have lost a child. It is surreal, to say the least.

Death is a natural part of life, a journey we all must take. Yet I always pictured my children laying me to rest, not the other way around. This is a club I never wished to join, and yet here I am. The journey has improved, but it continues.

Amber, I will never have enough words to express how proud I am to walk this path of healing with you after losing everything we once considered normal. When I asked if you would share your experience, you did not hesitate. You simply said, "Yes, it will help someone."

Thank you, sweetheart—my Dutchess, my reason to keep going. Always remember it is okay to fall, but how you rise is the true measure of your resilience and strength. Learn the lesson, and cast your cares on our Savior, Jesus. Let Him guide every aspect of your life.

To my Cross Barriers: Many of you were present for my 49th Birthday—New Beginning Celebration at my home in 2019. Though still broken, I was pressing forward, and you insisted on honoring me with a celebration that acknowledged my efforts to rise above my pain. Your kindness remains one of the greatest gifts I have ever received.

To my maternal brother and sister, Renaldo Smith, and Mynjuan Smith: You both were my motivation to excel. Beyond my roles as a servant of God, wife, and mother, the most significant role of my life was being Big Sister. I often joke that you were an afterthought because of our age difference, yet I inadvertently became a protector, teacher, and mother figure. These responsibilities shaped me into the woman I am today.

Little Brother, your story is still being written. I pray that God grants me the longevity to witness you walk fully in your divine purpose.

Little Sister, my heart breaks that you departed before I could complete this book. I am forever grateful to have been chosen as your big sister. I vividly recall breathing life back into your body when you were just a few months old. The medical staff told us my quick thinking saved your life. LIFE—such a precious gift. Like my son, I never imagined burying you. I am forever thankful that my face and hand were there as you transitioned.

Thank you for the 37 years—13,531 days. Thank you for allowing me to witness your authentic soul and radiant smile. I will carry your last words to our family with me, words spoken as difficult decisions had to be made: "My sister will do what's right by me, even with tears in her eyes." I will honor you and ensure that your treasured possessions, Jamora and Robert, are cared for. I love you.

To my mother, Eliza Jane Bitticks: Despite everything, I am because of you. By God's grace, our stories have become inseparably connected, stretching all the way back to the very beginning of your life. Who would have known that in telling mine, I would also be telling yours?

I can never fully grasp the depth of your grief. Your mother, the late Jessie Lee, passed away just one day after bringing you into this world. You were raised by your grandmother, the late Sue Edward Passmore—my beloved Grandmamama—a woman grieving the loss of her daughter while stepping up to care for her grandchildren: you and your brother, the late Lewis Edward Bitticks, Sr.

I remember when Grandmamama passed away. It changed you. Losing the only mother you had ever known marked the beginning of many painful chapters. Life didn't spare you from heartbreak—losing your brother, then your first grandchild, and eventually your own daughter. Loss after loss, trauma layered upon trauma... and yet, somehow, you kept going. You kept breathing. You kept loving.

To my Mother-in-Love, Mildred Lou Stennis Nofles—my Naomi: Words will never be enough to express the depth of my love and gratitude for you. From the very beginning, you embraced me—not as an in-law, but as your own daughter. In every hardship I've faced, you've stood by my side with the steadfastness of a guardian angel. You were there—not just physically, but deeply present—with grace, prayer, and love that anchored me through every storm.

Like Naomi in the Bible, your wisdom, compassion, and unwavering spirit have guided me through life's uncertain paths. And like Ruth, I chose to cleave to you—not out of obligation, but out of a love born of truth, loyalty, and divine connection. Where you go, my heart follows.

Your integrity, your courage in standing for what is right, your ability to lead with quiet strength—these are qualities I strive to mirror. You are a beacon, lighting the way not just for me, but for all who are blessed to know you. Forever your baby Ruth. With love beyond words.

To Charles L. Ward III: Your story is still being written, and I've come to understand that every journey is shaped by the paths we feel called to walk—even when those paths lead us apart. What once felt like abandonment to Amber and me may have been, for you, the space needed to find peace, healing, and truth. It didn't make the pain any less, but I no longer carry it as blame. I carry it as part of the story that shaped us into who we are.

Despite everything, I will always cherish what we shared as husband and wife. You weren't just my partner; you were my best friend and the only one

I ever trusted with the deepest parts of myself. Through the heartbreak, you also taught me that I am stronger than I ever gave myself credit for.

If this memoir ever reaches you, I hope you read it with compassion—for yourself, for us, and for the many layers of loss that have marked your life: your father, the late Charles L. Ward, Jr.; your grandfather, the late Charles L. Ward, Sr.; and our precious son, the late Charles L. Ward, IV. Each of these losses carved deeply within us and shaped the way we love, mourn, and move forward.

And still, I must say this: I am not a mother without you. I am not Glammy without you. And the same is true for you. We made each other through all the beauty and the sorrow. Although our journey didn't lead us to the happily-ever-after we once dreamed of, we remain family—forever. In spirit, in blood, in memory. Together, always.

INTRODUCTION

Beyond the Break: A Story We Didn't Ask to Tell

There are stories we don't ask to tell. They find us in our loss, our silence, our faith. This is one of those stories.

A Message to the Reader

If you're holding this book with tears in your eyes, questions in your heart, or silence on your lips, this is for you. Grief doesn't play fair. It interrupts. It confuses. It demands your energy and offers no map. We didn't write this to preach to you. We wrote this to sit with you.

- You are not too broken.
- You are not too late.
- You are not alone.

Maybe you've lost someone suddenly. Maybe you're losing yourself a little more each day. Maybe you're holding it together while quietly unraveling. You don't have to do this in secret.

You don't need permission to feel. If no one has told you lately, you are allowed to hurt. You are allowed to heal. You are allowed to hope for joy again. This is not the end of your story. Even if you're in the middle of the break. There is still beauty on the other side.

PART ONE
ANDERAL'S JOURNEY

"Even in this,
God will get the glory."

ANDERAL'S JOURNEY: ECHOES OF A LIFE

Finding out I was pregnant with my son was unforgettable. I smile even now, thinking he was already hinting at the joy he would bring into our lives before he was even formed. It was a cool winter day in Newport News, Virginia, when I learned I was expecting CJ.

My day had started out like any other—school first, then work at the Shoe Department in the local mall. I was greeting customers and stocking shelves when suddenly, everything went black. I had passed out.

No one knew what was wrong. My supervisor called my husband, who rushed me to the hospital at Fort Eustis, Virginia. The doctor ran all sorts of tests but finally smiled and said, "There's nothing wrong—just a little pregnant."

I was thrilled, and so was my husband. I can still hear his words: "I don't know whether to kiss you, pick you up, or what." Then he scooped me up and carried me to our car.

We didn't have the luxury of a baby shower to prepare for our son's arrival, but we did everything we could to make sure our firstborn had what he needed. I am forever grateful for the sacrifices my husband made to provide for us.

During the pregnancy, I faced complications from family stress, work, and school. My blood pressure rose so high that my doctor warned I was at risk of losing the baby. I was only five months pregnant at the time, and I still remember the concern on my husband's face. He looked at me and said firmly, "You are quitting your job."

This was extremely hard for me. As the manager of our home, I knew from the start that my husband's salary as a Specialist in the United States Army would not be enough to cover all of our financial obligations on its own. I looked at our situation and told him we needed to cut as many unnecessary expenses as possible if we wanted to stay comfortable.

He made the difficult decision to sell his prized possession—his 1989 white Volkswagen Jetta—and take on two part-time jobs. That car carried so many memories, including our first road trip to Virginia as husband and wife.

After selling it, we finally had enough to reduce our expenses and purchase everything we needed for the arrival of our firstborn.

The day of CJ's birth was far from ordinary. My husband had just finished a 24-hour duty shift and came home in time to take me to my weekly OBGYN appointment. Everything seemed routine until the doctor checked me. He asked how I was feeling, and when I told him I felt fine, he looked at both of us and said, "You're in active labor."

My poor husband was exhausted and ready for sleep—but our son had other plans.

At first, labor progressed normally, but then the medical team began having trouble monitoring CJ's heart rate. The doctor decided to place a monitor inside the womb. I agreed, but my comfort quickly shifted when the nurse that oversaw my care told me to hurry up so she could go take care of another patient.

I politely told her she would need to wait until my contraction was over. She dismissed me, insisting she wasn't waiting. She obnoxiously said, "You weren't waiting when you were getting it!" As she tried to insert the device, despite my request, I gathered every ounce of strength I had and kicked her away, shouting, "I SAID WAIT!"

My husband was so shocked that I had kicked the nurse and he immediately apologized on my behalf. But I stood my ground. I told him to find me another nurse—one with compassion and patience.

Once the internal monitor was inserted, I was observed for several hours without any progress. I only dilated to five centimeters. The doctor and nurses grew concerned, unsure what to make of the situation.

I remember the doctor turning to my husband and me, saying he didn't think the little fellow wanted to come out. It felt like CJ was playing peek-a-boo with the doctor. Each time the doctor said, "I see his head!" I could feel my baby pulling back into his previous spot.

It makes me laugh now, but at the time I was about to lose my mind. Eventually, the doctor decided to perform a C-section. My son finally made his entrance—by force—at 04:58 on August 10, 1995.

I never imagined I could love another human being as much as I loved my son.

CJ was a jokester—witty, curious, and endlessly affectionate. To know him was to love him. When I returned to school and work, I never had to worry about childcare. His godparents and nanny were always eager to have him.

I can still remember how often they would tell me not to rush to pick him up because he was so well-behaved. I never doubted he was being cared for, especially since he genuinely loved spending time with them. Even so, I usually declined their offers to keep him overnight. I wanted to be the last face he saw before drifting off to sleep and the first one he saw when he woke in the morning.

THE LABYRINTH OF LOSS: WHERE EVERYTHING SHIFTED

The months leading up to CJ's death carried a different kind of anticipation—the joy of preparing for Cahlil's arrival. CJ was both excited and nervous about becoming a father, but he embraced the role fully, determined to be a great one. He worked hard, poured himself into his music, and still held onto his dream of following in his father's footsteps by joining the military.

I still have the last messages he sent me. On February 26, 2017, he wrote: "Hello, My Queen, baby shower is at the VFW..." Two days later, on the 28th, I texted him about getting pictures taken.

"Yes Ma'am, what time?" he replied.

"4ish. You get a haircut?" I asked.

"I got to get one in the morning," he responded.

On March 1, I text: "Hope you enjoyed the photo shoot... I enjoyed it despite the cold...." He never replied.

On Sunday, March 5, at 8 a.m., I texted him: "My Prince, TT Tracee sent Cahlil a stroller and carrier, along with a pack and play, monitor, diapers, and wipes...." That same weekend, we had shared what would become our last meal together.

On March 6, 2017, I called him to say good morning, but there was no answer. I tried again at noon—still nothing. A nervous feeling crept over me. At 3:34 p.m., I sent him a message: "Hello Son...."

One minute later, at 3:35 p.m., his reply came through:

"Bye mom... Call 911... I'm sorry for every mistake I made in life. Please don't hate me...."

My heart stopped. I was so confused. I called 911 from my work phone, texted his father, and tried to call my son. I fled my office, texting and driving, desperate to get to his apartment.

When I arrived, police were already at the door. I texted, "Nothing is worth you harming yourself, please baby, open the door..." I begged the officer to break the damn door down. I felt a piece of me leave as they entered.

They came back to me and said, "Your son is dead." There was no empathy, no support in that moment.

I waited while the coroner removed him. They carried him out in a black body bag. I somehow held on to the bag as they placed it in the ambulance. My Prince. My firstborn. He was gone. He would never meet his son. He would never dance with me again. He would never see his sister graduate or get married. He would never...

The days that followed were a blur. Family arrived, and arrangements had to be made, but I was not okay. I went to the doctor and was prescribed medication to help with my nerves and to sleep. I wanted to wake up and have it all be a bad dream, but day after day—until his wake and memorial service—my reality was the same. My Prince. My baby. He was gone.

When CJ died, my soul didn't just break; it splintered in every direction. And with it, the fragile pieces of my life collapsed: the role of mother as I once knew it, the marriage I fought to sustain, the woman I thought I was. Every structure I'd leaned on for stability crumbled at once. This wasn't just heartbreak; it was an identity crisis wrapped in grief. I didn't just lose my child. I lost my future with him. I lost the version of my marriage I had prayed would endure. I lost the safety of predictability—the constant I thought would walk me through my golden years.

What followed felt like wandering blind through a maze built from memory, disappointment, and silence. Every step invited a new emotion: anger, sadness, numbness, rage — sometimes all within the same hour.

That's why I call it a labyrinth: grief, when layered, has no shortcuts. You can't climb over it or reason your way through it. You must walk every winding path — and I did, not because I was strong but because there was nowhere else to go.

MY PILLARS OF SUPPORT

Even in devastation, I refused to surrender hope. I believed that something could live in the ruins. As Genesis 50:20 says, "You intended to harm me, but God intended it for good." This part of my story isn't the triumph; it's the terrain — the soul fracture before the soul rebuild. My life has never been a fairy tale. It has been marked by turmoil that still makes me ask God, "Why me?" Yet I wouldn't change it because every struggle shaped me into who I am today. Through it all, God always gave me a cross to bear, and He never left me without strength.

I've had many supports along the way. My first spiritual father, Reverend Eugene Leonard, gave me the foundation of who I am in Christ Jesus. My best friend crew" my closest friends from my hometown motivated each other to succeed — failure was never an option. Our mantra, which I still hold close, was: "Nothing succeeds success but success itself." Together, we overcame challenges, and I believe we've touched the edge of the sky with our dreams and ambitions, still pressing forward to meet God's purpose. My best friends at Alabama State University pushed me too, even when I was "Ma Sha" to them all, devoted to self-growth and elevation.

My first mentor, the late Patricia Adebisi, pushed me to thrive and never allowed me to doubt that I was just as capable as anyone else. My high school counselor, Becky Wilson, taught me to recognize the beauty within myself.

She encouraged me to take advanced classes and prepare for college, even when I hadn't considered it.

The late Ida Romine was the first to teach me and others to take pride in our heritage and culture. She brought together other Divine Nine Auxiliary youth groups, and through that involvement, many of us were exposed to college campuses for the first time. Although she was a member of Zeta Phi Beta Sorority, she became the reason I chose Delta Sigma Theta Sorority.

I was also shaped by many other supports: my military families, colleagues, line sisters, and Sorors—all of whom carried me forward in different ways.

MY LEGACY OF INTEGRITY

Through all the turmoil, I found purpose in passing on the values that helped me endure. I like to believe I gave my children the same kind of balance and boundaries that my supports once gave me. I taught them to love God, live with integrity, and reach beyond their potential in every part of life.

Each school year, I had them create mission statements with goals and sign contracts to reinforce their commitment. I still have Amber do this to this day, as well as my late sister's children. My personal heartbreak forged a fierce commitment to building a legacy of strength and purpose for them— a foundation I pray will hold steady even when life shifts.

ANDERAL'S PERSPECTIVE: THE LABYRINTH OF LOSS

While everyone's experience with grief is unique, many find themselves moving through similar emotional landscapes. For me, the immediate aftermath brought deep shock and disbelief. It felt like a terrible nightmare

I would one day wake from. But as time passed, I realized the life I knew was gone.

Even though I longed for reassurance that it was all a dream, I came to understand that I had to keep moving if I didn't want to lose myself completely. Only a few people stayed connected and gave me enough strength to reach the place I am today. I not only lost my son, but I also lost what I believed would always be my constant—my husband of more than twenty-five years.

Although it would be easy to condemn my ex for leaving my daughter and me at the most vulnerable time of our lives, I choose instead to show grace and mercy, just as God shows us again and again.

Still, I will say a few things. Thank you for choosing me to be the mother of your children—for without you, I would not be Mother or Glammy. Thank you for loving the unapologetically me. Thank you for the life lessons. You always told me I was stronger than I realized, and now I understand that part of this journey was to prove it to myself.

Losing it all is painful, but rebuilding on the foundation God placed in me at the tender age of nine has shown me the power of trusting Him in all things. I have learned to be bold enough to believe that His Word will never return void. The journey itself is necessary to rise toward the fullness of God's purpose in our lives.

For that, I am eternally grateful—not only for being your wife but also for carrying the honor of continuing your legacy.

Thank you for trusting me to lead our family while you were away—not by choice but by duty to our country, defending us from harm on American soil. Each deployment felt like a loss of self and a struggle to remain the person I fell in love with and chose to love despite everything.

You are still enough, and you deserve the best God has to offer. I am sorry I wasn't enough to help him on the journey he must complete with the Creator.

After losing my son to suicide, losing my husband and our family unit was the second-worst thing I have endured. I believe his inner struggles, born of many losses, will find calm only when he looks at himself honestly, accepts his faults, forgives himself, and seeks true forgiveness from those he left behind.

Even the finality of the arrangements felt surreal, a stark contrast to the vibrant life of my beloved son. It was almost impossible to reconcile the energetic, loving boy I knew with the silence he left behind. In those first hours and days, a heavy fog of shock descended—a natural response to pain too great to comprehend.

It felt as though my mind fought to accept the truth, much like the disbelief described in scripture when devastating news first arrives. The Bible speaks to such sorrow: "When Nehemiah heard of Jerusalem's devastation, he sat down and wept. For some days I mourned." —Nehemiah 1:4.

In those early moments, the promise that "The Lord is close to the brokenhearted and saves those who are crushed in spirit." —Psalm 34:18, became a fragile source of comfort, a reminder that even in numbness, I was not abandoned.

As a mother, my grief was all-consuming, but I also witnessed my daughter, Amber, grapple with the loss of her only sibling—her first friend. Though our paths through pain were distinct, the absence of CJ created a shared void that bound us in unspoken understanding.

I watched her navigate a grief that was both personal and connected to the family we once knew. Her pain as a sister reflected a part of my own, reminding me of the depth of CJ's influence on every corner of our lives. That shared experience of loss—felt differently yet together—allowed us to connect on a deeper level, united by the irreplaceable absence of a brother and a son.

As reality began to settle in, anger surfaced—fierce, irrational, and directed at everything: the situation, the perceived unfairness, and at times, even at myself. A surge of frustration rose within me, accompanied by the constant, aching question: why?

When the shock began to fade, it gave way to a tidal wave of pain, often tangled with sharp edges of guilt and an endless loop of what ifs. This stage, common in grief, felt like a desperate attempt to rewrite a reality that could never be undone.

Scripture speaks to this depth of anguish:

"My heart is in anguish within me; the terrors of death have fallen upon me." —Psalm 55:4

In those torturous moments, the gentle reminder to "Cast all your anxiety on Him because He cares for you." —1 Peter 5:7 became a necessary anchor.

It was a confusing and unsettling emotion. Alongside the anger, I found myself caught in the if onlys—the mental bargains where I desperately tried to negotiate with a reality already etched in stone.

The Bible acknowledges the reality of anger:

"Be angry, and do not sin." —Psalm 4:4

Yet it also guides us toward hope and trust that reach beyond our immediate understanding:

"Why, my soul, are you downcast? Why so disturbed within me? Put your hope in God." —Psalm 42:5

As seconds turned into minutes, minutes into hours, hours into days, days into weeks, weeks into months, and months into years, a heavy cloak of sadness settled over me. This was not just fleeting grief. It was a deep weariness that made even the simplest tasks feel monumental. The vibrancy of life seemed to fade, leaving only a stark and isolating silence.

In those dark times, the comforting words of Psalm 23 became a beacon of hope:

"The Lord is my shepherd; He restores my soul."

And the wisdom of Ecclesiastes 4:9–10 reminded me of the strength found in others:

"Two are better than one, for if they fall, one will lift up his fellow."

These promises highlighted the importance of leaning on loved ones and the faith community when the weight of loneliness felt unbearable.

This stage often comes with what ifs and frantic attempts to bargain with a higher power—or with yourself. I replayed moments over and over: If only I had said this... If only we had done that. It is a natural human response to try to make sense of the senseless, to imagine undoing the unbearable.

I still struggle with this. My education taught me to focus on what lies within my circle of influence but knowing that did not make the journey easier. In my mind I ruminated on what should have been, what could have been, and what was truly happening. I should have stopped this. I should have, I should have, I should have.

It consumed me daily. For years I lived in a state of defeat, replaying every choice I had made about my son's upbringing—even though I had given him everything I had not been given as a child. In my head, it was never enough. I thought I could have done more, and I thought I should have.

Throughout this process, my attempts at bargaining with God were both profound and complex. My prayers reached beyond my son; I also pleaded for the preservation of my twenty-five-year marriage, which had already been facing strain before his passing. Over the years, our relationship had weathered betrayal trauma, miscarriage, deployments, and illness.

Despite having overcome so many challenges, we could not withstand the crushing grief of losing our firstborn and only son together. I recognize that each of us carried this loss in our own way, and my hope remains that he finds peace as he continues his own path of reflection.

The act of bargaining was more than wishful thinking—it was a heartfelt plea for stability in a season of distress. The collapse of my marriage at such a critical time revealed how difficult it is to endure profound hardship without steady support.

The symptoms we named—crying most of the day, losing interest in activities I once enjoyed, shifts in appetite or weight, disrupted sleep, and difficulty thinking or concentrating—became very real for me at different points.

LIVING THE LOSS, CARRYING THE LOVE

Acceptance does not mean being "okay" with what happened. It is about acknowledging the reality of the loss and learning how to carry it within my life. This process is gradual and uneven, not a single destination, and the ache will always remain. Instead, it is about finding ways to keep his memory present, carrying his love forward while allowing space for a fragile hope for the future—even on days when the pain returns with startling force. Over time, there has also been a growing understanding of how to live with this loss.

In the beginning, shock was all-consuming, a protective shield that kept me from facing the full weight of the tragedy. It appeared as numbness, confusion, and an inability to take in what had happened.

This stage, as I understand it, is about learning to navigate a "new normal"—testing my limits and discovering what I am capable of in the face of such a profound loss. It is the slow work of finding my footing again in a world that feels permanently altered.

In this process, the words of Jesus became a steady source of strength: "In this world you will have trouble. But take heart! I have overcome the world" (John 16:33). Alongside this, the assurance of Romans 8:28—that "in all things God works for the good of those who love him"—remains a firm foundation of hope, even in the midst of enduring sorrow.

PILLARS OF HEALING

ANDERAL'S CHURCH ADDRESS: A MESSAGE OF HOPE AND HEALING

Church family, this is personal for me. I can't give my full testimony in the time allowed, so I'll share the cliff notes. Amen.

On March 6, 2017, my family as I knew it was shaken to its core. My beloved firstborn, Charles Leonard Ward IV—affectionately known as CJ—died by suicide. I speak his name often to confront the enemy and declare that even in this, God's perfect plan and purpose remain. Even in this, his life will bring healing. Even in this, mindsets are being renewed with purpose—on purpose—for God's glory. God will continue to receive the praise. Even in this. Hallelujah.

Many ask, were there signs? No. That is not our family's story. If there were signs, CJ hid them well from us.

Depression is real. It is a mental health condition known as a mood disorder. These disorders occur when shifts in mood extend beyond the normal ups and downs of daily life. Episodes of depression last for at least two weeks, though at times they can stretch into months or even years.

Parents, guardians, and educators—our children face pressures that differ from those we once knew. Their circumstances are not the same as ours were. Those of us who have walked with God for some time understand that in the middle of the storm, we must trust Him even when we cannot trace His hand. But our children are not there yet. They need us to be present—not through the things we can buy or the distractions we can offer, but through our presence. They don't need stuff. They need us.

Real talk. My kids were both raised in church and given a strong foundation that led them to give their lives to God at an early age. But what do you do when faced with a situation like the one I was in? My seventeen-year-old baby, after losing her first friend, her best friend, and only brother, looked at me and asked, "Why did God take my brother?"

How do you answer a question like that? The truth is, I couldn't. I was wrestling with the same questions—struggling to understand God's logic and timing myself.

So, what do you do when you know the right things to do, yet they don't seem to work for you? I went to my pastors for support—for myself and my husband at the time. I also spoke with my daughter's youth pastors and encouraged her to share her heart with them as well.

What I learned in that moment is that our spiritual growth and our mental health growth are not the same. Amber and I had to do our work individually, and that was necessary. Despite all the specialized education I had in my area of expertise, it did not help me, nor was I able to help my daughter. Our spiritual leaders gave us the guidance we needed to strengthen our spirits, but it was our therapists who helped us rebuild our mental health so we could face the trauma—our depression, the sense of abandonment I felt from my ex, and the weight of grief.

God became whatever we needed Him to be. That truth carried us to our "But God" moment. We were weak, but God is strong and mighty. We lost people and things, but God supplies all our needs according to His riches in glory. But God renews our spirit daily. But God. I cannot and will not lack, because my Father owns it all.

Amber Bre'naee Ward—and the woman who stands before you today—represents our "And God" state. Promise kept. All things have come together just as the Word declared. My baby is prayers answered. She graduated high school only two months after my CJ's death by suicide.

Despite grieving the loss of her brother, the family unit she had always known, and battling depression, she went on to graduate from the University of Central Oklahoma on time. Today, she is pursuing her master's at the University of Oklahoma. We are still working daily to become the best versions of ourselves.

Takeaways: Please do not hear what I am not saying. I believe wholeheartedly in the power of prayer. But we cannot fight the multitude of mental health challenges with prayer alone. Our pastors cannot do this work by themselves. They need the partnership of mental health professionals. We must approach the complexity of mental health with an all-hands-on-deck commitment.

Let our pastors focus on growing us spiritually while mental health professionals address our mental well-being. I believe that partnership is key to confronting mental health challenges.

To the children listening: it is okay not to be okay. Don't let anyone tell you otherwise. Your concerns, feelings, and emotions are valid. If life ever pushes you into despair, don't make a permanent decision based on temporary emotions.

Parents, validate your children's concerns when they try to tell you what's troubling their spirit. Remember, we have lived longer than our children and some of them don't yet have the words to explain how they feel. Those feelings can show up as behavioral issues at school, self-harm, or even thoughts of suicide—signs that need our attention and care.

Parents, be open to the information others share with you about your children. Sometimes, others notice signs of struggle long before you do. Early intervention is key to knowing how to involve the right support systems. Remember, not everything is an attack on you or your child. Release that defensiveness and choose growth instead.

A LETTER TO MY GRANDSON, CAHLIL

My dearest, Cahlil,

I know it's hard to carry a hole in your heart for someone you love so deeply, especially since you never got the chance to meet him. Your dad was an incredible person, and I want to tell you about him so you can know who he was. His name was Charles Leonard Ward IV, but everyone who loved him called him CJ. He carried the name of the men in your family who came before him: your grandfather, G-Pa Charles Leonard Ward III; your great-grandfather, Charles Leonard Ward, Jr.; and your great-great-grandfather, Charles Leonard Ward, Sr. That legacy now belongs to you, too.

Your dad had a kindness so genuine that he never met a stranger. He always looked for the good in people and was quick to help anyone in need. His joy was undeniable, and he loved his family and friends with his whole heart. In many ways, he was just like you. He was a happy child who loved to laugh, and his witty smile could brighten any room he entered.

He was also very talented and creative. He played the saxophone and loved basketball. He was so good that, in the seventh grade, he earned a special letter for his skills. But his greatest passion was music. He almost always had a pen and paper in his hand, writing lyrics and creating songs. Music became his safe place—a way to pour out everything he was feeling inside.

I also want you to know how truly excited he was to be a dad. He would often talk to Auntie Amber and me about how much he already loved you, even before you were born. His heart was overflowing with joy, and he dreamed of all the things he would teach you and the fun you would share. He was ready for every moment of fatherhood, and he carried so much love for you in advance of the life you would have together.

When your dad was alive, he was dealing with a sickness of the mind. It was a serious illness that caused him pain we could not see on the outside. That illness led him to do something we cannot fully understand, but it was not your fault. Nothing you said, nothing you did, and nothing you thought caused this. You are a good boy, and your dad loved you very, very much.

I want you to know your heart is safe with us. We are your family and your support for life. We believe God has given us the gift of loving your dad through you. When you smile that witty smile of yours, it reminds us of him. When you are kind to others, we see his generous heart. Your mannerisms and your personality are like his. His love lives on in you. We will keep his memory alive by telling stories and celebrating the wonderful person he was.

He is with God now, and God is holding him — and God is holding you, too. When you are sad, or angry, or have questions, please come and tell me. I love you, and I will always be here for you.

Together Always,
Glammy

Photo Credit: TopFlight Productions, Shelton Moore

PART TWO
AMBER'S JOURNEY

"The day my world changed forever."

AMBER'S JOURNEY: THE DAY THE WORLD TURNED UPSIDE DOWN

I'll be honest: I never thought I would have the strength to talk about this tragedy in my life. Still, I know that my words—and my mother's—may help someone facing the same pain we endured. The journey doesn't end; grief comes in waves. It rises and falls, and sometimes it hits without warning.

Grief looks different for everyone, and there is no single right way to grieve a loved one. When you lose someone, it can feel as if a part of you dies with them. That is how I felt when I lost my best friend, my big brother, and my only sibling to suicide. This is my story.

THE LAST HUG: A MEMORY ETCHED IN MARCH

March 2017—the month and year that changed everything for me. It started out on a high note. On March 1st, my family took new pictures together. It had been a long time coming; the last family photos we had were from 2007. Back then, I was nine and CJ was twelve. Now, I was eighteen, and CJ was twenty-one.

My mom had begged us to take these pictures, while my dad and CJ complained, as they always did, because they hated photo sessions. To make matters worse, the weather that day was freezing and windy, which gave them even more reason to grumble.

We went to three different locations for our photoshoot, snapping countless pictures. But one stood out above all the rest. In that moment, CJ jumped into my dad's arms with a huge smile stretched across his face. That picture became my favorite, and it was truly priceless.

Photo Credit: The Shutter Sisters

My mom and I were laughing too, because of course CJ would be the one to jump into Dad's arms—he had always been the silly one. Even my dad was smiling, which was rare since he hardly ever did. I will always remember that day, CJ's smile, and his laughter.

March 5th was the last day I saw my brother. He came over to the house, and we played video games together in my dad's man cave. We played Call of Duty: Black Ops, and as usual, CJ was beating me. I could never aim the gun to save my life, so I often used ballistic knives instead. CJ insisted that I was cheating and told me I had to use the guns.

I grew up with my dad always reminding me that guns were not toys. He told me how dangerous they were and that they were nothing to play with. He would often say that he could never forgive himself if anything ever happened to me or my brother, CJ.

I remember CJ sharing how excited he was to be a dad, though he admitted he was nervous too. He said, "Little sis, I just want to be a great dad to my son." I reassured him, telling him that he would be an amazing father, and that Cahlil would love him deeply. I reminded him that our family would be there to support him, and I told him, "You are not alone."

One day, we walked downstairs and CJ went into my parents' closet. I heard my dad yell, "Boy, get out of my stuff!" CJ just laughed as he walked out of the room. He was always messing with my dad's things, especially his shoes and clothes. My dad wore a size nine shoe, while CJ wore a size twelve. Still, CJ always tried to put on my dad's shoes, even though they were way too small. Stubborn as ever, he insisted on squeezing his big feet into them. It became his little routine whenever he came over to the house.

CJ hugged me and told me that he loved me. His hug was much tighter than it usually was. At that moment, I felt like something was wrong, but I could not have predicted what would happen next.

MARCH 6TH, 2017: THE UNRAVELING

March 6th, 2017, the day my world turned upside down. I remember it like it was yesterday.

That morning felt ordinary. I went to school, sat through all my classes, and came home. Everything seemed fine—or at least that's what I thought then. I went to my room and turned on the TV. Around 3:00 p.m., my phone rang. It was my mom.

The moment I heard her voice; I could tell something was wrong. There was panic and worry in her tone as she explained that she was on her way to CJ's apartment. She had received a strange text from him.

The message said he was sorry for everything he had put her through, and at the end, he wrote just one word: "bye." That word wasn't normal for our family. To us, "bye" meant forever. Because my dad served in the military and was often deployed, our family made a point to say "see you later" instead. We even had our own phrase we used all the time: "together always." That's why the word "bye" unsettled my mom so deeply.

She told me she would call once she reached CJ's apartment. I told her I loved her and waited for the phone to ring again.

An hour passed—still nothing from my mom. No calls, no texts. That's when the worry set in.

I tried calling and texting her, but there was no response. I called my dad, and again, nothing. My chest felt tight. Finally, I called my big sister Juju. (You'll hear a lot about Juju throughout my story—she was like a sister to me and became a rock during this time.)

Juju answered, and the moment I heard her voice, I broke down crying. I told her something was wrong and that no one was picking up their phone. She asked, "Do you have the car at the house?" I told her yes, and that I was going to drive over to CJ's apartment by myself. Juju said she had to get off the phone because she was at work, but she asked me to let her know as soon as I got there.

I remember driving in complete silence. On the way there, my volleyball coach called me. It confused me at first—my season was already over, so I didn't expect to hear from her.

I answered the phone, and it was Coach Alisha, who was also my youth pastor's wife. She asked, "Hey, what are you doing?"

I told her I was on my way to CJ's apartment because something didn't feel right and no one was answering their phone. Alisha told me to call her as soon as I got there. I promised I would.

When I hung up, I was even more unsettled. Why was she calling me now, of all times? I couldn't make sense of it. I drove the rest of the way in silence, repeating to myself that I just needed to get there.

I turned into CJ's apartment complex and immediately noticed several police cars and ambulances. No one was outside. I started looking for my mom and dad, but I couldn't see my mom's car or my dad's motorcycle.

Tears began to well up because I had no idea what was happening. Juju called me back. I told her I couldn't find anyone and that I didn't know what was going on.

As I was talking to her, I saw my dad walking toward me on the sidewalk. I told Juju I had to call her back and ran to meet him.

I asked him what was happening. My dad looked at me with a straight, blank face and said, "CJ is dead."

I stared at him in disbelief. "No, that's not true—we saw him yesterday!" I screamed.

He repeated it, but I couldn't process the words. I kept shouting, "No, that's not true! My big brother is still alive!"

As I was talking with my dad, Alisha, my volleyball coach, pulled into the apartment complex. It made sense now—my mom had called her to stay with me at the house until they got home, but I was already gone.

I called Juju back from the car. I had left my car at the apartment complex because I couldn't drive at that point. When Juju answered, I told her that CJ was dead. She looked at me in disbelief and asked what had happened. I told her we didn't know anything yet.

We began to cry together, both of us in utter shock. CJ was gone.

I remember scrolling through my phone and seeing that my dad was on Facebook Live. On the live stream, he was clearly distraught. He told the world that CJ was dead, that he no longer believed in God, and that he was the last of the Ward generation. My dad's father and grandfather, the I and II, had already passed. My dad was the III, and CJ was the IV.

After my dad posted the live video, my phone started blowing up with texts and calls. I was overwhelmed. Everyone was asking, "Why?" or "What happened?" I had no answers for anyone because I didn't even have the answers for myself yet.

I remember coming home and seeing a line of cars in the driveway. Inside, many faces greeted me, including bonus aunts and uncles who had become part of our family through my dad's military service.

I walked upstairs to my dad's man cave and saw broken wood chips from the TV dinner table—it was shattered, as if my dad had broken it in frustration. I sat on the couch, thinking over and over that this couldn't be happening, that it was just a bad dream.

Eventually, everyone left, and the house fell silent once more. I didn't sleep at all that night. At this point, we still didn't know the cause of CJ's death.

I remember being on my phone and seeing that Riley was on Facebook. Riley went to school with me, and we shared something important: we had both lost our big brothers. Riley lost his brother Alec in 2013, and I remember how devastated our school and community were when he passed. CJ and Alec had been good friends, so his loss had affected CJ deeply as well. Both were loved by many.

That night, I reached out to Riley, knowing he would understand exactly how I felt. He had heard from another classmate that CJ was gone, so when I messaged him, he responded immediately. I remember our conversation vividly. He was honest with me, telling me that losing my brother would be a rough journey and that I needed to grieve instead of trying to stay strong for everyone. He admitted that this was something he wished he had done himself—allowed himself to grieve instead of carrying the weight of appearing strong. I told him I would try my best, and he reassured me that he was here for me whenever I needed to talk.

I tried to sleep that night but couldn't. I stayed up until the sun came up, lost in thought and grief.

MARCH 7TH, 2017: THE TRUTH REVEALED

I went to school. You might be wondering why I even went the day after losing my brother. Honestly, I just did not want to be alone, so I decided to go. Normally, I would blast music while driving, but that morning I drove in complete silence. Bags hung under my eyes from not sleeping, and I had my hoodie pulled up over my head.

When I arrived at school and, I sat in my car for a moment. A van pulled up, and Ms. Felicia stepped out. She had been like a bonus mom to me while I was at school, and her cooking was amazing. I got out of the car and greeted her. Ms. Felicia could always tell when something was wrong. She asked softly, "What's wrong, sweetie?"

I broke down and told her that CJ was gone, and we still didn't know what had happened. She told me I should not be at school, but I explained that I just needed to get out of the house. She hugged me and reminded me that she loved me.

I walked down the halls of my high school with my hood pulled over my head. When I entered morning care in the cafeteria, I sat at a table, earphones in, and put my head down. A hand touched my shoulder—it was my history teacher, reminding me to take my hood off. I reluctantly complied and rested my head for a few more minutes.

When I looked up, I saw my best friend Ebbie walking through the door. Our eyes met, and I ran to her. We collapsed onto the floor, sobbing together. I had known Ebbie since kindergarten, so CJ had been like a big brother to her too.

I remember crying on the floor with Ebbie when a woman from the office knelt beside us. She looked at me and said she was sorry for my loss, but that I should be grateful for the time God had given us with my big brother. I almost forgot to mention—I went to a private Christian school. I remember feeling so angry when she said this. I wanted to scream at her that it wasn't enough time. Instead, I just stared at her in disbelief and got up from the floor.

It felt like everyone at school came to me. "I'm here for you," "Sorry for your loss," and "You and your family are in my prayers"—these were just a few of the many things I heard. I became overwhelmed, so Ebbie and I left and went to the park. We stayed there for a while, just trying to keep our minds busy.

I got a call from my mom, telling me I needed to come home. I dropped Ebbie back off at school and rushed to the house. When I walked in, my parents were in the living room with Pastor Heath and Alisha. They told me they had just learned the cause of CJ's death. They looked at me and said, "CJ died by suicide." Suicide—a word rarely spoken, and mental health for that matter—echoed in my mind.

I stared in disbelief. I did not want to believe that my big brother, my only sibling, had died by suicide. CJ had always been a giver, always silly, and always smiling. He was loved by many. I could not believe what I was hearing. I remember telling my parents that they must be mistaken. My mind wandered, and I sat in silence, trying to grasp it all. The question of "how" hung heavy, a painful mystery that compounded the shock.

For the next few days, our house was full of family members who came into town. People brought meals so we could eat and drink, though I hardly had an appetite. I barely ate. My big sister Juju and her family were the first to arrive. The Trotters have been like a second family to me since sixth grade. Julianna (Juju) had met my brother first—they both went to Eisenhower together.

It's funny, CJ had a crush on Juju. I remember it was Easter Sunday when Juju came to the door to ask my brother if he wanted to ride bikes in the neighborhood. I had not met Juju yet. I walked up to the door and told CJ to introduce me. He told me to go away, but Juju interrupted him and said, "Let me meet her." I stepped under my brother's arm, said hi, and told her my name was Amber. From that moment on, Juju and I were inseparable.

Back to the story—Juju and her family arrived first. I remember running to Juju as soon as I saw her, collapsing into her arms, and crying together. She never left my side during this time, and I am forever grateful to have her as a bonus sister.

They say people have villages that help them through life's trials and tribulations. I have a great village. Juju is one of those people, along with Jerald, Izzy, Eboneisha, the Powell family, my volleyball coaches—Coach Amanda and Coach Alisha—the Trotter family, the Gattenby family, the Hamilton family, the Keys, the Fishers, and many more. I am forever grateful to these people who are my village and an important part of my life.

As I mentioned, losing CJ really hurt me and changed me forever. I do not know what I would have done without my village during this extremely challenging time for me and my family.

MARCH 15TH, THE REALIZATION

March 15th was the day I truly realized my brother was gone. It was CJ's wake. I remember waking up that morning next to Juju, upstairs in my dad's man cave. My eyes were swollen from crying the night before, and I hadn't slept at all. Juju kept encouraging me to rest, but I couldn't. I was too anxious about what the day would bring.

"The Lord is close to the brokenhearted and saves those who are crushed in spirit." —Psalm 34:18

As I've mentioned before, my brother died by suicide. He shot himself. I didn't know what to expect what he would look like, or if he would even still look like himself. That was my biggest fear.

I got dressed slowly, still crying. Juju looked at me and said, "We are in this together, little sis. I'm here for you, no matter what." I hugged her tightly and told her I loved her. Before I knew it, we were on the way to the funeral home.

When we arrived, I froze. I couldn't stop crying and didn't want to get out of the car. Juju squeezed my hand and told me to take a deep breath. Together, we stepped out.

Inside, CJ's song, Chase'n A Dream, was playing. A slideshow of family photos ran on the screen to the right. I sat for a while, trying to gather the strength to go up front and see him. Juju stayed with me, saying she'd walk with me when I was ready. But I wasn't ready. I kept thinking this had to be a nightmare—that any minute, I'd wake up.

Finally, Juju stood and reached for my hand. We walked down the aisle together. That's when I saw the casket for the first time. It hit me hard. Caskets mean death. That means it's real. That means the end.

My mom and Juju's mom followed behind us. When I reached the casket, I saw my brother my first best friend lying there. I dropped to the floor and sobbed. My mom rushed to hold me as I screamed, "No, not my brother!"

"Blessed are those who mourn, for they shall be comforted." – Matthew 5:4

Eventually, I stood again, tears still running down my face. CJ looked like he was just sleeping. He still looked like himself. He wore a royal blue shirt, one of his favorite colors, and a patterned tie. I looked at him and whispered, "I love you."

As more people came to pay their respects—friends, cousins, extended family the rest of the day blurred together. But one thing stayed with me: my big brother was really gone.

Romans 8:38–39 (NIV)

"For I am convinced that neither death nor life, neither angels nor demons, neither the present nor the future, nor any powers, neither height nor depth, nor anything else in all creation will be able to separate us from the love of God that is in Christ Jesus our Lord."

MARCH 16TH: TOGETHER ALWAYS

March 16th was the day my world changed forever—the day I said goodbye to my brother, CJ, my best friend, my only sibling. Sitting in that church, I expected to be overwhelmed with tears, but instead, I felt nothing. I was numb. It was as if my heart had shut down, trying to shield me from a reality that was too heavy to bear.

Deep inside, though, a single thought kept echoing: I should have saved him. I kept asking myself what I had missed, what I could have done differently, why my love hadn't been enough to ease the pain he carried in silence. That thought still haunts me.

As I looked around, I realized I wasn't alone in my grief. The church was full, every pew holding someone whose life CJ had touched—friends, family, neighbors, and classmates all gathered to honor him. The sight of so many faces was both heartbreaking and comforting, proof that my brother had left an imprint far deeper than he probably ever realized.

When my youth pastor, Pastor Heath, stood to give the eulogy, I held on to his words like lifelines. He painted a picture of CJ's spirit exactly as I remembered it: loving, kind, and impossibly goofy. He spoke of CJ's ability to make people feel special, to bring light into a room just by walking into it. For a brief moment, I could almost hear his laugh again, that familiar sound that could brighten even the darkest days.

After the service, I witnessed something I will never forget. My dad, who had managed to stay composed throughout the ceremony, suddenly collapsed. Family friends had to carry him out. When he came to, he broke down completely. It was the first time I had ever seen my father unravel, the first time I truly saw the weight of CJ's death break him. In that moment, I understood just how deeply my brother was loved—not just by me, but by every single person in that room, and especially by our dad.

I miss CJ with every breath I take—the inside jokes, the laughter, the quiet moments of simply being together. His absence has left a hole in my heart that nothing else can fill. And yet, even in this pain, I know that the love I have for him is unshakable. It will never fade, never weaken. I will carry him with me for the rest of my life. I will love him forever. Together always.

THE AFTERMATH: WHEN SILENCE CAME

No one ever talks about the true beginning of grief. For me, my journey didn't start the moment my brother died, at the wake, or even at the funeral. It started after it all ended. My grief began when everything became SILENT. The silence was deafening—not peaceful or comforting, but heavy and suffocating. In those quiet moments, the weight of reality pressed down on me. That is when it truly hit me: CJ was gone, and nothing would ever be the same again.

Everyone left, and it was just us—me and my family—trying to navigate the reality of our new normal. Some days, I could feel completely okay; other days, I was an emotional wreck. Grief comes in waves and never follows a plan. Little memories or objects could trigger it. My brother was an artist who wrote songs, and I couldn't even listen to them. Hearing his voice was too much, a reminder that I would never hear it again. Days went on, and I questioned everything. I even questioned my relationship with God. I couldn't understand the why behind this tragedy.

I was raised in a good Christian household. We went to church, served in the community, and tried to be kind and good people. And yet, this still happened to our family—the unimaginable. I couldn't understand how God could allow this. The word that kept coming to mind was simple but heavy: "Why?" Why didn't God protect our family? Why didn't He protect CJ? These questions consumed me.

All the Bible verses I had grown up reciting—verses about God's protection, His plan for us—suddenly felt hollow. As much as I wanted to hold on to them and believe, all I could feel was betrayal and anger. Months went by: April, May.

MAY: GRADUATION WITHOUT HIM

Senior year was not supposed to end like this. It had started off great: senior pictures, winning the state championship with my volleyball team, spirit week, and more. Nothing could have prepared me for the reality that my big brother would not be at my high school graduation.

I was in the yearbook club, and my senior classmates and I were in charge of the senior pages. Being in yearbook allowed me to create my own page, and before CJ died, I had asked him to write a message for it. This is what he wrote:

"Amber, It's hard to believe that you are about to walk the stage! I am so happy, but I am sad at the same time because I can't call you my "baby sis" no more. Nevertheless, you will forever and always be my "baby sis," there is no time in the world that will change your place in my heart.... Even through our ups and downs, I am so proud of you "baby sis," Bubba loves you so much." Together Always CJ

MAY 13, 2017

The day I had been waiting for was finally here — my high school graduation. Since I attended a small private school, our graduation was very intimate. There were only ten people in my class, which allowed us to do things most public schools couldn't. One of those traditions was creating senior boards for graduation.

The senior boards featured childhood pictures, high school accomplishments, and fun facts. As I worked on mine and looked through childhood photos, one thing stood out: my brother was always there with me. There are very few pictures of me alone. Another tradition at our graduation was having our families come up to the front while the principal prayed over us.

The moment came during graduation when the principal asked our families to come forward. I watched as everyone's family walked up, and my heart sank—CJ was not there. I immediately broke down at the front. My mom and dad held me as I cried, and I could not get over the fact that my big brother wasn't there.

I had always imagined CJ being extra and goofy in the crowd, holding a big sign and shouting, "Let's go, Baby Sis!" I know he was there in spirit, but it wasn't enough. Even so, I kept thinking about how I had made it through. Just two months after losing my brother, I had somehow managed to finish high school despite the tragedy that had hit our family.

WHEN JOY AND SORROW SHARE THE SAME SPACE

After my graduation, my volleyball family congratulated me, and my two coaches, Coach Alisha and Coach Amanda, told me they had a gift for me. They said they waited to give it to me afterward because they knew it would make me emotional.

We walked outside, and I opened the gift. Inside was a beautiful canvas—a picture of me and CJ, one of the last photos we took together during our family pictures. I immediately started crying and thanked them both. They hugged me and told me they loved me and wanted me to have a piece of CJ wherever I went to college.

I had been accepted into several colleges, but I ultimately chose the University of Central Oklahoma in Edmond. The school was close enough to come home when I wanted, but far enough to allow me to start fresh. That canvas reminded me that, even as I stepped into a new chapter, I was not leaving CJ behind. It came with me when I moved into my dorm, propped up against the wall as a quiet piece of home.

I thought college would feel like a fresh start—and in some ways, it did. But grief does not respect fresh starts. It followed me onto campus, into every classroom, every late night, every quiet walk back to my dorm. While other freshmen were busy making friends, decorating their rooms, and planning their new lives, I carried this invisible weight. No one around me knew the story behind my tired eyes or why some days felt unbearable.

I smiled when people asked how I was adjusting, but deep down, I was struggling to exist in this new space without him. I would look around and see brothers visiting their sisters on campus or families celebrating move-in day together, and each time it felt like another crack in my chest. CJ should have been there—teasing me about college life, maybe helping me carry boxes, or giving me a hard time about being on my own. Instead, I only had his picture and the silence of what should have been. College did not erase my grief.

If anything, it magnified it. College placed me in a world where everyone else seemed to be moving forward, while I was still stuck in the aftermath of loss. I carried CJ into that new space—not as a living presence, but as an ache that refused to be left behind.

Slowly but surely, I started to get into the rhythm of college life. Thankfully, I was not completely alone when I first arrived. My best friend Jerald was there, which made me feel a little more at home. Jerald and I attended freshman orientation over the summer, and that is where we met Shelby. We instantly clicked, and just like that, she became part of our friend group. Shelby and I ended up in the same dorm, though on different floors. She, Jerald, and my roommate Lauren all became very close to me. We did everything together, and before long, they were not just friends—they were my family away from home. They were the people I ate meals with, studied with, stayed up too late with, and leaned on when the days felt too heavy.

Next came Jarrett. I met him in psychology class, and we quickly realized we were also living in the same dorm. It felt like one of those "meant to be" moments, because before long, Jarrett became part of our circle too. He fit right in, and together we formed a small, close-knit group—people who showed up for one another, making the hard days lighter and the good days even better.

Even with my grief still so heavy and consuming, I found myself having moments I did not think I would ever experience again. Moments where I actually laughed—not the forced kind you give when someone tells a joke you don't really feel like hearing, but real, genuine laughter that came from deep inside. I smiled without guilt. I made memories that felt good, even with the ache of CJ's absence still pressing on my chest.

It did not erase the pain—nothing could—but my college family gave me space to breathe again. They reminded me that joy and grief could coexist, that it was okay to hold both at once. With them, I felt safe enough to release the heaviness at times, but I also learned it was okay to let the light back in.

ANOTHER LOSS

Just when I thought I was learning to navigate my grief, something else happened. It was October 2017—fall break—and I had to go home. I was already dreading the trip because Lawton no longer felt the same after losing my big brother. The town felt cold and unfamiliar.

My dad picked me up from college. I got in the car, and he hugged me, asking how I was doing. I told him I was managing that I was starting to really like college and my new friends. The drive to Lawton seemed endless.

I was listening to music as my dad drove when he suddenly looked at me and said he had to tell me something. My heart started pounding as I braced for what was coming. I could never have predicted his next words: divorce. My dad told me that he and my mom were getting divorced. Just like that, another layer of grief was added. Losing my brother was not enough—I had to lose my family unit too?

I looked out the window, staring at the sky, and thought, "Okay God, what else?" I could not believe what I was hearing. It had not even been a year since CJ passed, and now this? I couldn't comprehend what was happening.

My dad spoke, but I disassociated from the moment. All I heard were my thoughts telling me that nothing would ever be the same. The divorce did not just mean two people separating—it meant home would never feel the same again. Holidays, family dinners, even the simple comfort of knowing both my parents would be in the same place... all of it was gone. I was grieving my brother, and now I had to grieve the family I once knew.

In that moment, my grief felt doubled. Not only was I missing CJ every single day, but I was also watching the version of my family that included all of us together slip through my fingers. It was another kind of death—the death of what once was—and it deepened the ache I was already carrying.

After hearing the news about my parents, I felt completely lost. All my life, my mom and dad had been the example of what love and commitment looked like. They had been married for over twenty years. To me, their marriage was supposed to be unshakable, the one constant I could depend on when everything else felt uncertain. How could something that lasted so long just vanish? How could two people who had built a life, raised children, and survived so much together suddenly decide to walk away from it all? I could not understand it.

The confusion ate at me. If even their love—the strongest love I thought I knew—could end, then what did that mean for my own future? Did love ever really last? Could I ever trust it for myself? Those questions ran in circles through my mind, slowly breaking down the way I saw the world.

I started to spiral. Already grieving CJ, I now felt like every piece of stability in my life was slipping away. My brother was gone, and now the safe image of my family was gone too. It felt like the ground was crumbling beneath me, with nothing to hold onto.

That is when I began to lose myself. I went down a dark path—one filled with anger, numbness, and choices I wish I had not made. I tried to distract myself from the pain in unhealthy ways, searching for something, anything, to fill the void. But no matter what I did, the emptiness remained.

The grief of losing my brother had already been unbearable, but adding the divorce on top of it felt like too much. I was no longer just grieving CJ; I was grieving the family I thought I had, the stability I thought would always be there, and the belief that love could be unshakable.

FINDING MY WAY BACK

After months of spiraling and feeling completely lost, I finally realized I could not keep carrying everything on my own. Losing CJ, watching my parents' marriage fall apart, trying to balance school while pretending I was okay—it was too much. I felt like I was drowning.

In that darkness, I pushed people away. Even Juju. She had always been my rock, but instead of leaning on her, I shut her out. I did not want her to see how broken I really was. I said things I regret, and I let the pain put distance between us. Eventually, she had to protect herself and cut me off. For six months, we barely spoke, and though it hurt, I was too far gone in my own grief to reach out. Looking back, that distance was one of the hardest parts of that season.

Eventually, I decided to try therapy. At first, I hated it. Sitting in a room, being asked to talk about feelings I had buried deep—it was uncomfortable. But slowly, I started to open up. I talked about my anger, my guilt, and the ache that would not let go of me. Therapy did not take away the pain, but it gave me tools to carry it differently. It taught me that healing did not mean forgetting CJ. It meant finding a way to live with his memory and still move forward.

As I started to heal, Juju and I found our way back to each other. It was not instant—we had some hard conversations, tears, and honesty—but we rekindled our sisterhood. We both realized that grief had already taken enough from us. Rebuilding with her was one of the most healing parts of my journey.

Therapy also opened the door for me to find my way back to God. For so long, I had been angry with Him. I could not understand how He allowed all this pain into my life, why He did not save CJ, or why He let my family fall apart. For a while, it felt easier to push Him away than to face those questions.

But slowly, I started to notice He had been there all along—in my friends who became my college family, in Juju when she came back into my life, in my counselor, and even in the strength that kept me breathing on the days I wanted to give up.

My faith started to feel real again—not perfect, not without doubt, but real. I learned that grief and faith can exist together, that I can question and still believe, that I can hurt and still hope. And in that tension, I started to find peace.

One verse I held onto during that season was Psalm 91:4:

"He will cover you with his feathers, and under his wings you will find refuge; his faithfulness will be your shield and rampart."

That verse gave me the image I needed—a God who was not distant, but close. A God who gathered me like a fragile bird and sheltered me under His wings. Even when I was angry with Him, even when I pushed Him away, He never stopped covering me. His faithfulness became the shield that protected me when I could not protect myself.

COLLEGE GRADUATION

If you had asked me during my first year of college whether I thought I would ever see graduation, I would have laughed—or maybe cried—and told you no. There were too many obstacles stacked against me: losing CJ, my parents' divorce, the nights I cried myself to sleep, the mornings I could barely drag myself out of bed. College was supposed to be about freedom and fun, about discovering who I was. Instead, it often felt like a battlefield, a place where I was fighting just to stay alive inside.

There were so many times I thought about quitting. Times I stared at assignments piling up, wondering how I could possibly care about deadlines when all I was trying to do was survive grief. Times I sat in class, distracted, feeling the weight of everything I had lost while everyone else seemed carefree. Times I questioned whether I had the strength to keep going at all. But somehow, I did.

It was not just me. It was God carrying me when I had no strength left. It was my therapist giving me tools to process what had felt impossible. It was my college friends who kept pulling me into life when all I wanted to do was hide. It was Juju and me finding our way back to each other after months of distance. Piece by piece, step by step, I made it through. Not perfectly. Not gracefully. But I made it.

By the time May 2021 came, it still did not feel real. I had done it—on time, exactly when I was supposed to—something I never thought would be possible in those dark early years. My graduation was not just about earning a degree; it was about surviving everything that had tried to break me.

That morning, as I slipped on my cap and gown, my heart was in two places. One part of me was proud, excited, and grateful. The other part was grieving all over again. I could not stop thinking about CJ. I pictured him in the stands, yelling my name louder than anyone else, probably embarrassing me in the way only a big brother can. I imagined how he would have hugged me afterward, squeezing me so tightly I could hardly breathe. His absence was louder than the cheering crowd that day. And yet, his presence was there too.

Sitting in that crowd was my nephew, Cahlil. He was so young, but he carried so much of CJ's spirit in him. His smile, his little expressions—they reminded me so much of my brother. Seeing him there felt like God had given me a gift, like a piece of CJ was with me on one of the biggest days of my life. I walked across that stage with tears in my eyes—not just because of the accomplishment, but because I knew CJ was with me in a different way.

After the ceremony, when I found my family in the crowd, my eyes went straight to Cahlil. I hugged him and felt a wave of peace. It did not take away the ache, but it softened it. It reminded me that CJ's story did not end with death—it lived on in the people he loved, especially in his son.

Looking back, graduation was more than a diploma or a ceremony. It was a victory. It was proof that grief had not won. Despite the pain, the setbacks, and the nights I thought I would not make it, I did.

That day reminded me of a verse that became etched on my heart:

"Those who sow with tears will reap with songs of joy." — Psalm 126:5

My college years had been sown with tears—endless tears. But on that May afternoon in 2021, standing there in my cap and gown, surrounded by family, with CJ's spirit alive in Cahlil, I reaped joy. Not a perfect, pain-free joy, but a hard-earned, sacred joy that comes only after walking through the valley and realizing God was there all along.

Graduation was not just an ending. It was a beginning—a reminder that even in the darkest seasons, God can bring new life, new hope, and new songs of joy.

Photo Credit: Amanda "Mandy" Esmon
Edits by: Topflight Productions (Shelton Moore)

A LETTER TO MY NEPHEW, CAHLIL

My sweet Cahlil,

From the moment you came into this world, you have been a light for our family. You remind me so much of your daddy—I see him in your smile, your laugh, and in the way you carry yourself without even realizing it. Having you in my life feels like having a piece of him still here, and I am so thankful for that.

I want you to always know how loved you are. Your daddy loved you more than anything, and if he were here, I know he would be bragging on you at every chance. He would be there to cheer you on, tease you, and tell you how proud he was. Even though he cannot be here physically, his love for you has not gone anywhere—it is in you, always.

I know there will be times when you feel the weight of him not being here, and those moments will be hard. But I want you to remember that you will never have to walk through life alone. You have me. You have a family who adores you. And you have God, who will carry you through every single step.

You have been such a blessing in my life, Cahlil. Watching you grow has given me hope on days I thought I had none left. You make me smile in ways I did not think I could again. You have shown me that even in deep pain, joy can still break through.

I promise I will always be here for you. I will tell you stories about your dad, remind you of who he was and how much he loved you, and be by your side through every season of your life.

You are my heart, my joy, and my forever reminder that love never dies. Together always.

Love,
Auntie Amber

Photo Credit: TopFlight Productions, Shelton Moore

THE UNBREAKABLE THREAD

Grief can feel like a severing, like someone you love has been pulled away, leaving only silence and longing. But imagine your connection to them as a golden thread, placed by God Himself. This thread stretches across time and eternity, linking your heart to theirs in a way that cannot be broken.

Even though you cannot see them, that thread still holds. It is anchored in a love stronger than death—a love that reaches beyond the grave, beyond pain, beyond separation. Just as nothing can separate us from the love of God, nothing can truly sever the bond you share with someone you have loved deeply.

This verse reminds us that love, especially love rooted in God, is eternal. The person you miss is not gone from your story; they remain part of it, always.

PART THREE
ANDERAL'S PATH

"Understanding Grief, Healing, and Resources."

THINGS TO UNDERSTAND

"This isn't a crisis of character. It's a crisis of care."
— Anderal Ward

Grief, as we experienced it, is complex and often non-linear, more like an irregular heartbeat or the unpredictable waves of the ocean than a straightforward progression. While models such as the five to seven stages developed by Elisabeth Kübler-Ross (denial, anger, bargaining, depression, and acceptance) provide frameworks for understanding, emotions often resurface and intertwine in unexpected ways. There is no magical solution or correct way to grieve; the journey requires taking "one step, one breath, one moment at a time" to navigate the emotional ups and downs. We view grief as a trauma of the heart, one that requires acknowledging pain and seeking holistic support.

Denial: A defense mechanism that protects us from the initial shock of loss. It can appear as disbelief or the feeling that this is not really happening.

Anger: Once the reality begins to set in, anger can surface. This might be directed at the person who died, at others, or even at oneself.

Bargaining: Often involves "what ifs" and attempts to negotiate with a higher power or with oneself to change the outcome.

Depression: A deep sadness and overwhelming sense of loss that goes beyond just feeling down. It can involve many of the symptoms we experienced, such as tearfulness, loss of interest, and changes in sleep and appetite.

Acceptance: This does not necessarily mean being okay with the loss but rather acknowledging its reality and learning to live with it.

Other researchers have identified Shock, the initial overwhelming reaction to loss, and Testing, a phase in which individuals may try to navigate their new reality and explore what they are capable of.

Moving through these stages is rarely straightforward. You might revisit earlier emotions or experience them in a different order. There is no right or wrong way to grieve. In this part of the book, I sincerely hope you will connect with your own experience—or with the experience of a loved one you are trying to support. Develop a mindset that this journey requires one step, one breath, one moment at a time to navigate the emotional rollercoaster of grief.

Remember, as Psalm 34:18 reminds us:

"The Lord is near to the brokenhearted and saves the crushed in spirit."

NAVIGATING GRIEF: A MOTHER'S AND DAUGHTER'S PERSPECTIVE

The journey through grief after losing CJ to suicide has been a landscape of shifting emotions and unexpected turns. It is not a straight path, but more like navigating a winding road—moments of clarity interspersed with stretches of overwhelming fog. We share some of what we have learned about grief, not as a rigid checklist, but as a way to understand the feelings that may arise.

Grief is not linear. It resembles the ocean's waves, with moments of calm followed by sudden, powerful surges of emotion. You may find yourself moving back and forth between different emotional states—a spiral of growth where each revisit brings deeper insight.

PART FOUR:
ANDERAL'S RESTORATION

*"Rebuilding the Heart—
Steps Toward Restoration
and Resilience."*

Grief shattered the structure of my life. But faith rebuilt the foundation. I didn't wake up whole. I woke up honest. That honesty became the first brick in my restoration. Piece by piece, I reclaimed trust, identity, safety, and rhythm. Not the same versions of what I lost, but new ones, forged in fire.

The five pillars that helped me begin again:

1. **Grief Acknowledgement** – Naming the trauma and its emotional truths.
2. **Faith Integration** – Leaning into scripture and spiritual reflection.
3. **Therapeutic Support** – Accepting help from professionals without shame.
4. **Community Anchoring** – Letting safe people hold my truth with care.
5. **Purpose Reclamation** – Letting loss fuel legacy, not silence.

This is my meaning of the five pillars that helped me.

Pillar 1: Grief Acknowledgement: Before I could heal, I had to speak the pain out loud. I had to admit: this hurts. Not just once, but deeply, constantly, without apology. I stopped hiding grief behind performance. I let it sit with me, walk with me, and break me open so it could also stretch me. Grief is not weakness; it's evidence of love. And naming it is the beginning of freedom.

"The Lord is close to the brokenhearted." —Psalm 34:18

Pillar 2: Faith Integration: My faith didn't remove grief; it carried me through it. I returned to scriptures I learned at age nine and chose to believe they still applied to me now. I prayed like Jesus did in Gethsemane: *"Take this cup."* I also surrendered, *"Not my will, but Yours."* Faith taught me that God can handle my brokenness. And healing became worship. *"Trust in the Lord with all your heart." -Proverbs 3:5*

Pillar 3: Therapeutic Support: God sent helpers in human form— counselors, pastors, support group leaders. Voices that didn't rush me but held space.

Therapy gave language to my heartbreak. It helped me understand grief not as madness, but as meaning. You can seek help and still be full of faith.

Jesus heals through both prayer and people. *"Plans fail for lack of counsel, but with many advisers they succeed." -Proverbs 15:22*

Pillar 4: Community Anchoring: Grief isolates—but I fought to stay connected. leaned into friendships, shared stories, and sat in spaces that allowed tears.

Not everyone knew what to say, but the ones who stayed were sacred. Healing happened when I let others into my ache. Together, we built belonging inside brokenness. *"Carry each other's burdens..." -Galatians 6:2*

Pillar 5: Purpose Reclamation: When pain nearly buried me, I dug deeper into purpose. I realized that legacy could be louder than loss. "Even In This" became a message. "Beyond the Break" became a movement. CJ's life became a light I would carry. Purpose gave me strength—not to erase the past, but to repurpose it for healing. "You intended to harm me, but God intended it for good..." —Genesis 50:20

This is the work of restoration. This is what healing looks like in motion.

I didn't climb out of despair—I crawled. Sometimes with a whisper. Sometimes with a scream. But always with hope. "Trust in the Lord with all your heart and lean not on your own understanding..." —Proverbs 3:5

I learned to breathe through the breakdown, to speak into the silence, to write my way toward becoming.

You can begin like this:

Dear Me, the one who is becoming,

This is your declaration. This is your dialogue with destiny. No judgment. No pressure. Just love in motion. Write as though your healing depends on hearing your own voice because it does. You are not just rebuilding. You are reclaiming every sacred part of who you were always meant to be.

THE IRREGULAR HEARTBEAT
OF GRIEF – ONE BREATH AT A TIME

There's no straight line through grief. It curves, twists, dips, and falters like a heart struggling to find its rhythm again. That's how I describe my grieving process—not clinical, not clean. It was an irregular heartbeat, one that skipped, stuttered, and sometimes threatened to stop. My education taught me about the five stages of grief—sometimes seven, depending on the theory but no classroom could have prepared me for how those stages feel when lived.

They don't follow rules. They don't take turns. They crash over one another. Grief is loud, yet sometimes nearly silent. You don't "graduate" from grief. You survive it—one step, one breath, one moment at a time. "Abba, Father," he said, "everything is possible for you.

Take this cup from me..." Mark 14:36

Bargaining consumed me—not just over my son's death, but over my marriage. I begged God to undo reality, to rewind time, to preserve our home, our bond, our vows. I reviewed every choice I had made as a mother. Even knowing I had given CJ everything I wasn't given, I asked: "Was it enough? Did I miss something? What could I have done?"

And my marriage—twenty-five years long was not spared. We had overcome so much: miscarriage, deployment, illness, betrayal. Yet we could not survive the weight of this loss. His journey diverged from mine, and my heart shattered again.

"So do not fear, for I am with you..." — Isaiah 41:10

Other than losing my son to suicide, losing my husband and the family we built was the second-greatest heartbreak I've endured. My world imploded—child, companion, covenant. And in the silence of abandonment, I chose grace.

A LETTER OF GRACE, NESTED IN HEALING

I will not vilify my ex-husband. He is still family. I choose instead to say: thank you for choosing me to be the mother of your children. Thank you for loving the unapologetic me. Thank you for showing me the strength you always said I had.

This loss became my proving ground. God reminded me that what He placed in me at age nine was enough—to believe in His promises, to rebuild on His foundation.

Know that you are still enough. You still deserve peace. I am sorry I could not walk you through the valley that now belongs to you and the Creator. You do not overcome grief by denying it. You overcome it by walking through it with honesty, prayer, and help.

I leaned on faith. I leaned on therapy. I leaned on friends brave enough to hold me in my truth. Grief is trauma of the heart, but healing is possible if you choose to breathe.

TRANSITION PASSAGE: FROM RESTORATION TO COMMUNAL RENEWAL

Faith rebuilt me. Therapy re-grounded me. Purpose redirected me. But healing wasn't just about me. It became about us—our families, our churches, our cultures, our conversations. As my heart began to regain its rhythm, I noticed something deeper: we are grieving silently in spaces meant to be sanctuaries.

We show up to Sunday service carrying buried pain, lead programs with hidden sadness, raise children while quietly breaking inside. So, I asked myself: how do we bring healing into the spaces where we live, worship, and lead? How do we stop treating mental health as a private shame and start seeing it as a collective calling?

This next chapter is not just an invitation; it's a summons—to break silence, create safe spaces, and build bridges between our faith and our emotional well-being. Because if restoration is possible in one soul, it is possible in many.

Grief may arrive personally, but it is carried communally. We often show up with heartbreak and no words, with deep pain and nowhere to lay it down. We keep showing up, wearing resilience like armor. But what if we stopped hiding our grief and began healing together? Shared grief doesn't mean comparing losses; it means recognizing every ache as sacred.

Shared grace doesn't mean earning compassion; it means offering it freely, because that's how we survive the unbearable. In our community, healing began not with answers, but with presence. Someone showed up. Someone cooked a meal. Someone sat beside us and did not rush the silence. And that grace? It multiplied.

Scripture Reflections:

- **Romans 12:15** – "Rejoice with those who rejoice; mourn with those who mourn."
- **2 Corinthians 1:3–4** – "So that we can comfort those in any trouble with the comfort we ourselves receive."
- **Galatians 6:2** – "Carry each other's burdens, and in this way you will fulfill the law of Christ."
- **Isaiah 61:3** – "To bestow on them a crown of beauty instead of ashes."
- **Psalm 147:3** – "He heals the brokenhearted and binds up their wounds."
- **Ecclesiastes 4:9–10** – "If either of them falls down, one can help the other up."

MENTAL HEALTH IN OUR COMMUNITIES

BREAKING BARRIERS, BUILDING BRIDGES

Mental health isn't just a diagnosis—it's a doorway. A doorway to healing. To honesty. To hope. But in many Black communities, that doorway has been barricaded—by stigma, by silence, and by systems that were not built with us in mind. We don't just know the statistics—we have lived the reality. Black men are hurting. Black boys are grieving. And too often, their pain is dismissed, misdiagnosed, or ignored.

We lost CJ not just to suicide, but to silence, to pressure, and to a system that did not make space for his full humanity. We speak his name because his story cannot be treated as an exception. It is a mirror. A ministry. A message.

What the Numbers Say

- Suicide rates among Black Americans rose 58% between 2011 and 2021.
- Black male students (grades 9–12) are more likely to attempt suicide than white male peers.
- Only 25% of Black adults seek mental health care, compared to 40% of white adults.
- Just 2% of psychologists in the U.S. are Black.
- Black adults below the poverty line report twice the emotional distress—yet often receive inadequate care.

These numbers are not abstract. They are anchored in the grief we carry, the gaps we witness, and the communities we serve.

Why These Disparities Persist

- **Stigma and Shame:** Mental health is still seen as weakness in many Black households and churches.

- **Historical Mistrust:** The medical system has failed and harmed us before—rightfully breeding skepticism.
- **Cultural Misdiagnosis:** Black boys and men are more likely to be labeled with aggression rather than distress.
- **Access Barriers:** Therapy is expensive, unfamiliar, and often unavailable in our neighborhoods.
- **Adultification:** Our sons are treated like grown men before they reach puberty—robbing them of tenderness and care.
- **Representation Gap:** A lack of Black mental health providers makes cultural understanding harder to find.

NAVIGATING THE UNIMAGINABLE: A COMPASSIONATE GUIDE TO SUICIDE, GRIEF, AND THE CHRISTIAN FAITH

The topic of suicide is often shrouded in silence, stigma, and sorrow—especially within the church. For centuries, it has been met with judgment rather than empathy. Yet as pastors, friends, family members, and therapists, we are called to bring light to the darkest corners of human suffering.

This chapter aims to serve as a compassionate guide: offering a framework for understanding, a pathway for communication, and a source of hope for anyone touched by suicide.

WHAT THE BIBLE SAYS (AND DOESN'T SAY) ABOUT SUICIDE

A common fear, often rooted in tradition rather than biblical scripture, is that suicide is an "unpardonable sin." When we turn to the Bible, we encounter a more complex picture—one that does not offer a single, clear-cut command against suicide, but instead reveals a God who is intimately acquainted with human pain.

The Bible records several instances of suicide, including Saul (1 Samuel 31:4), his armor-bearer (1 Samuel 31:5), Ahithophel (2 Samuel 17:23), and Judas Iscariot (Matthew 27:5). Each account is a tragic narrative of despair, defeat, or guilt. Significantly, the text presents these events as tragedies without explicitly condemning the individuals to damnation for the act itself. This distinction is crucial. The Bible's central message of salvation is that we are saved by grace through faith in Jesus Christ (Ephesians 2:8–9), not by the manner of our death.

The act of suicide is not a rejection of God in a final moment; rather, it is often a desperate response to overwhelming mental, emotional, or physical pain. For Christians, salvation is a state of being—a relationship with God that cannot be broken by a single, desperate act. We can have confidence in God's mercy and sovereignty, trusting that He is the ultimate judge who sees the heart, the pain, and the brokenness.

UNPACKING MYTHS AND BIASES WITH CLINICAL INSIGHT

The silence surrounding suicide is often perpetuated by pervasive myths and biases. Addressing these head-on is a critical step toward creating a truly compassionate and supportive community.

Myth: Suicide is a sign of weak faith.

Truth: This is perhaps the most damaging myth. Mental health professionals recognize that suicidal thoughts are a symptom, not a character flaw. They often result from treatable medical conditions such as Major Depressive Disorder, Bipolar Disorder, PTSD, or severe anxiety. These conditions can change brain chemistry and affect cognitive function, making it difficult for a person to see a way out of their pain. Equating suicide with a lack of faith is not only inaccurate—it can also shame individuals into hiding their struggles, making them less likely to seek life-saving help.

Myth: Talking about suicide plants the idea in someone's head.

Truth: The opposite is true. Open, honest conversation is one of the most powerful tools for prevention. Mental health experts consistently advise that asking someone directly if they are having suicidal thoughts can reduce their risk. This directness shows you care, gives them a chance to share their pain, and can be the first step toward finding help. Silence and secrecy are what allow despair to grow.

Myth: If they truly trusted God, they would not be depressed.

Truth: This bias confuses faith with a constant state of emotional well-being. Clinically, depression is a complex condition influenced by genetics, neurobiology, and environmental factors. Faith and professional help are not mutually exclusive. A person can have deep, abiding faith in God while also needing medical treatment, therapy, or medication to address a mental health condition. Encouraging professional help is a way of stewarding the resources God has provided for healing.

SPEAKING WITH A CHILD ABOUT A PARENT'S SUICIDE

When a child loses a parent to suicide, it is a trauma of the deepest kind. The conversations that follow must be handled with immense care, honesty, and love.

HOW TO TALK TO A CHILD WHO HAS LOST A PARENT TO SUICIDE

When a child is grieving a suicide loss, what we say—and what we don't say—matters. Our words can either bring healing or add to their confusion and pain. Here are some guidelines based on clinical research and biblical principles.

What to Say (and Why):

"This was not your fault." Repeat this phrase often. Experts in child trauma say this is the single most important message a grieving child needs to hear. The child's brain is wired to look for a reason for the pain, and they will naturally assume it is their own.

"It's okay to feel sad, angry, or confused." Validate their emotions. This aligns with Jesus's own grief and human emotion, showing that feelings are part of our experience and do not separate us from God. (John 11:35)

"I love you, and I am here for you no matter what." This provides a sense of safety and stability in a world that has been turned upside down.

"God loves you and is with you even when it hurts." Reassure them of God's constant presence, drawing on passages like Psalm 34:18, which says, "The LORD is close to the brokenhearted."

What NOT to Say (and Why):

"Everything happens for a reason." While this may be a comfort to some adults, it can imply to a child that their parent's suicide was part of a plan, which can make God seem cruel.

"God just needed another angel." This statement can create fear and anxiety, making the child wonder if God will take other people they love. It also misrepresents the nature of angels in Christian theology.

"Don't cry" or "Be strong." This teaches the child that their emotions are unacceptable and forces them to suppress their grief, which can lead to long-term psychological and emotional issues.

Avoid complex or overly theological explanations. Keep it simple and focused on love and reassurance.

WHEN THERE ARE NO SIGNS

Perhaps the most baffling and painful aspect of suicide is when it happens without warning. For the loved ones left behind, the absence of clear signs can trigger an agonizing cycle of self-blame: "What did I miss? Why didn't I see it?"

Mental health professionals recognize that many individuals who die by suicide are highly skilled at hiding their pain. Some experience what is sometimes called "high-functioning depression," maintaining a veneer of normalcy while suffering internally. Their struggle is often invisible to the outside world—a silent battle that rages behind a brave smile.

For pastors, friends, and family members, the most important response is self-forgiveness. You are not to blame. You cannot be expected to see what was intentionally hidden. Rather than getting stuck in the "Why?"—a question that may never be fully answered—it is more constructive to focus on the "What now?"

- **What now for the grieving family?** Offer tangible support: meals, childcare, a listening ear.
- **What now for our community?** Learn from this tragedy and commit to making mental health a priority, fostering a culture of open conversation and support.
- **What now for my own grief?** Seek professional grief counseling for survivors. It is a vital step toward healing.

THE IMPORTANCE OF PASTORAL CARE AND PROFESSIONAL COUNSELING

In the wake of a suicide, pastoral care and professional counseling are not separate; they are intertwined, essential for holistic healing. Pastors and faith leaders, as spiritual caregivers, are often the first to be called in times of crisis.

Your role is invaluable: to provide spiritual comfort, offer biblical perspective on suffering, and be a steady presence of Christ's love. Yet, the pastoral role is not meant to replace the clinical expertise of a trained mental health professional.

Mental health challenges such as depression, PTSD, and suicidal ideation are complex medical conditions, not spiritual failures. Addressing them effectively requires both spiritual guidance and clinical support.

Pastoral Care provides the spiritual foundation:

It offers comfort through scripture, prayer, and the support of a faith community. It can help a person reconcile their grief with their faith, find hope in God's promises, and place their pain within a larger spiritual narrative. It is about caring for the soul, providing compassion and presence that can only be experienced in a loving community.

Professional Counseling provides the clinical expertise:

A licensed therapist or counselor can use evidence-based techniques to help individuals process trauma, develop coping strategies, and manage the symptoms of mental health conditions. They are equipped to navigate intense emotions that pastoral care alone may not fully address, including the neurological and psychological impacts of grief and trauma.

Pastors, your most powerful act of care may be to lead the way in destigmatizing mental health by modeling and encouraging parishioners to seek professional support. Referring someone to a Christian counselor or a therapist who respects their faith is not a sign of failure; it is a demonstration of deep understanding of holistic well-being—mind, body, and spirit.

RESOURCES AND PROFESSIONAL HELP

While faith provides a foundational source of hope, it is essential to utilize the clinical resources available. If you or someone you know is in crisis, please seek professional help immediately.

- **Crisis & Suicide Prevention Hotlines:** These services are free, confidential, and available 24/7.
- **Mental Health Professionals:**
- **Therapists/Counselors:** Provide talk therapy to help individuals process thoughts, emotions, and behaviors.
- **Psychologists:** Specialize in the study of behavior and mental processes, often providing therapy and psychological testing.
- **Psychiatrists:** Medical doctors who can diagnose mental health conditions and prescribe medication.

The Christian faith does not provide easy answers to the "Why" of suicide, but it offers profound hope for the "What now?" It reminds us that God is a God of grace, mercy, and deep compassion, present even in our darkest moments. He mourns with us and, through His Spirit, offers a path toward healing and hope for those left behind.

FAITH + THERAPY: A SACRED PARTNERSHIP

We believe in prayer. We also believe in professional help. And we believe God can work in both. Faith without action is incomplete, and healing without truth is limited. It's time to stop telling our children to "just pray it away." It's time to stop asking pastors to fix what therapists are trained to address. Let's build churches that nurture both soul and mind.

CJ was raised in the Word, but even faith-filled families need emotional literacy and mental health support. Our story shows that a spiritual foundation must be paired with mental health care—and that our culture must evolve to reflect this reality.

Scripture Reflections

- "The Lord is near to the brokenhearted and saves the crushed in spirit."
- Psalm 34:18
- "Plans fail for lack of counsel, but with many advisers they succeed."
- Proverbs 15:22
- "He has sent me to bind up the brokenhearted." -Isaiah 61:1
- "Carry each other's burdens." -Galatians 6:2

CLOSING REFLECTIONS: "EVEN AFTER THE BREAK"

If you've made it to this page, thank you. You didn't just read our story. You felt it. Grief is messy. Healing is holy. And neither is linear.

You have permission to:

- Heal slowly.
- Laugh again.
- Still believe in joy
- Ask for help—and deserve it.

Your story is not done. Even in this, you are still held.

BEYOND THE BREAK: FINDING HOPE AND HEALING

The journey of grief is deeply personal and non-linear, often feeling like a spiral where emotions resurface and intertwine. It reflects the depth of love and connection, and there is no prescribed route or checklist to follow. We hope our story encourages you to embrace your unique path one step, one breath, one moment at a time.

If you or someone you know is struggling with suicidal thoughts, please remember that help is available and recovery is possible. Support, including therapy and, when appropriate, medication, can provide essential care for mental health conditions.

Resources for help include the 988 Suicide & Crisis Lifeline: call or text 988 anytime in the U.S. and Canada. In the U.K., you can call 111. You can also reach the Crisis Text Line by texting HOME to 741741 from anywhere in the U.S., at any time, about any type of crisis.

Remember, suicide is complex and rarely caused by a single factor. Warning signs and risk factors often exist, and reaching out can make a real difference. You are not alone.

REFERENCES

American Foundation for Suicide Prevention. (n.d.). *Books for loss survivors*. Retrieved from https://afsp.org/books-for-loss-survivors/

American Foundation for Suicide Prevention. (n.d.). *Ethical reporting*. Retrieved from https://afsp.org/ethicalreporting/

Amy Lou Jenkins. (n.d.). *Multiple perspectives in memoirs*. Retrieved from https://amyloujenkins.com/multiple-perspectives-in-memoirs/

Book Printing China. (n.d.). *How to create a compelling memoir book*. Retrieved from https://www.bookprintingchina.com/blog/how-to-create-a-compelling-memoir-book

Brainz Magazine. (n.d.). *6 essential steps to masterful memoir storytelling and unlock your life's narrative*. Retrieved from https://www.brainzmagazine.com/post/6-essential-steps-to-masterful-memoir-storytelling-and-unlock-your-life-s-narrative

BubbleCow. (n.d.). *Memoir editing*. Retrieved from https://bubblecow.com/blog/memoir-editing

Counseling.org. (n.d.). *The historical roots of racial disparities in the mental health system*. Retrieved from https://www.counseling.org/publications/counseling-today-magazine/article-archive/article/legacy/the-historical-roots-of-racial-disparities-in-the-mental-health-system

David Kessler Training. (n.d.). *Writing through loss*. Retrieved from https://www.davidkesslertraining.com/writing-through-loss-2025

DMH Los Angeles County. (n.d.). *Suicide prevention*. Retrieved from https://dmh.lacounty.gov/mental-health-resources/suicide-prevention/

Electric Literature. (n.d.). *Grief memoirs are for the living*. Retrieved from https://electricliterature.com/grief-memoirs-are-for-the-living/

Goodreads. (n.d.). *Memorial days*. Retrieved from https://www.goodreads.com/book/show/212806569-memorial-days

Heal With CFTE. (n.d.). *Storytelling and healing*. Retrieved from https://www.healwithcfte.org/blog/storytelling-and-healing

Hersmile.org. (n.d.). *Grief is not linear: Embracing the twists and turns*. Retrieved from https://hersmile.org/grief-is-not-linear-embracing-the-twists-and-turns/

Jane Friedman. (n.d.). *Memoir: Common mistakes*. Retrieved from https://janefriedman.com/memoir-common-mistakes/

Jane Friedman. (n.d.). *POV in memoir*. Retrieved from https://janefriedman.com/pov-in-memoir/

Marion Roach. (n.d.). *Writing good transitions*. Retrieved from https://marionroach.com/2014/07/writing-good-transitions/

Maven. (n.d.). *Storytelling techniques*. Retrieved from https://maven.com/articles/storytelling-techniques

McLean Hospital. (n.d.). *Black mental health*. Retrieved from https://www.mcleanhospital.org/essential/black-mental-health

Mental Health America. (n.d.). *African mental health: Historical context and cultural beliefs*. Retrieved from https://mhanational.org/resources/african-mental-health-historical-context-and-cultural-beliefs/

Memento. (n.d.). *Writing to heal trauma: Narrative writing for emotional healing*. Retrieved from https://meminto.com/blog/writing-to-heal-trauma-narrative-writing-for-emotional-healing/

Minority Health. (n.d.). *Mental and behavioral health - Black/African Americans*. Retrieved from https://minorityhealth.hhs.gov/mental-and-behavioral-health-blackafrican-americans

NAMI. (n.d.). *Your journey: Identity and cultural dimensions / Black/African American*. Retrieved from https://www.nami.org/your-journey/identity-and-cultural-dimensions/black-african-american/

National Center for Biotechnology Information. (n.d.). *[Title of article related to PMC3418821]*. Retrieved from https://pmc.ncbi.nlm.nih.gov/articles/PMC3418821/

ReportingOnSuicide.org. (n.d.). *Recommendations*. Retrieved from https://reportingonsuicide.org/recommendations/

Samaritans. (n.d.). *Suicide and self-harm literature FINAL*. Retrieved from https://www.samaritans.org/documents/607/Suicide_and_self_harm_Literature_FINAL.pdf

School of Public Health, University of Michigan. (n.d.). *Black mental health disparities*. Retrieved from https://sph.umich.edu/pursuit/2024posts/black-mental-health-disparities-2024.html

Upbility.net. (n.d.). *Grief, loss, coping, and advice*. Retrieved from https://upbility.net/blogs/news/grief-loss-coping-and-advice

University of Essex. (n.d.). *[Title of article related to ESJ article ID 399]*. Retrieved from https://publications.essex.ac.uk/esj/article/id/399/

World Health Organization. (n.d.). *Suicide prevention for journalists*. Retrieved from https://www.who.int/docs/default-source/mental-health/suicide-prevention-journalists.pdf

Writer.org. (n.d.). *Memoir year with Nicole Chung*. Retrieved from https://writer.org/event/memoir-year-with-nicole-chung/

Writer's Digest. (n.d.). *14 techniques to write emotional truth to engage readers: Why it works and how in successful storytelling.* Retrieved from https://www.writersdigest.com/write-better-fiction/14-techniques-to-write-emotional-truth-to-engage-readers-why-it-works-and-how-in-successful-storytelling

American Academy of Pediatrics. (2023). *Suicide rates spike among Black adolescents.* https://www.aap.org

Centers for Disease Control and Prevention. (2024). *Suicide data and trends.* https://www.cdc.gov/suicide

KFF. (2024). *Mental health care disparities.* https://www.kff.org

National Alliance on Mental Illness. (2024). *Black/African American mental health.* https://www.nami.org

Office of Minority Health. (2024). *Behavioral health data for African Americans.* https://minorityhealth.hhs.gov

Substance Abuse and Mental Health Services Administration. (2023). *Grief and trauma support resources.* https://www.samhsa.gov

USC Suzanne Dworak-Peck School of Social Work. (2019). *Mental health stigma in the Black community.* https://dworakpeck.usc.edu

Verywell Mind. (2020). *Mental health stigma by culture.* https://www.verywellmind.com

The Holy Bible, New International Version. (2011). Zondervan.

Ward, A. D. (2025). *Beyond the break: A journey of grief, grace, and healing.* Welcome To The Storm Publishing!™

American Foundation for Suicide Prevention. (2023). *Talking to children about suicide loss.* https://afsp.org/talking-to-children-about-suicide-loss

American Psychological Association. (2020). *Publication manual of the American Psychological Association* (7th ed.). American Psychological Association.

Office of Minority Health. (2024). *Behavioral health data for African Americans.* https://minorityhealth.hhs.gov

Substance Abuse and Mental Health Services Administration. (2023). *Grief and trauma support resources.* https://www.samhsa.gov

The Holy Bible, English Standard Version. (2001). Crossway Bibles.

The National Child Traumatic Stress Network. (2022). *Caring for children after a disaster, death, or violence.* https://www.nctsn.org/resources/caring-children-after-disaster-death-or-violence

University of Southern California Suzanne Dworak-Peck School of Social Work. (2019). *Mental health stigma in the Black community.* https://dworakpeck.usc.edu

Verywell Mind. (2020). *Mental health stigma by culture.* https://www.verywellmind.com

Zucherman, J. (2020). *Pastoral care and counseling in a post-modern world.* NavPress.

ABOUT THE AUTHOR

Ms. Anderal DeShawn Bitticks-Trammell Ward is the Founder and CEO of Even In This Enterprise, LLC. She is a seasoned leader, educator, community catalyst with over 20 years of dedicated service addressing intimate partner violence, sexual assault, and child abuse. Her career spans both military and civilian sectors, where she has consistently supported survivors through compassionate care, strategic coordination, and trauma informed education.

In her role as a Legal Administrative Specialist within the military justice system, Anderal has provided critical support to victims and witnesses navigating complex legal processes. Her work includes coordinating services, conducting legal research, facilitating multidisciplinary trainings, and developing innovative case management systems that strengthen victim support across her areas of responsibility. Her contributions reflect a deep understanding of trauma, advocacy, and systemic care, shaped by years of hands-on experience and specialized training.

A proud alumna of Anniston High School in Anniston, Alabama, Alabama State University in Montgomery, Alabama, Cameron University in Lawton, Oklahoma, and the University of Oklahoma in Norman,

Oklahoma, Anderal's academic journey reflects a steadfast commitment to personal growth and purposeful service. She earned a Bachelor of Science in Sociology with a minor in Psychology and a Master's degree in Human Relations. Her extensive training in resilience building, trauma response, and financial literacy equips her to serve diverse communities with clarity, compassion, and excellence.

She is also a proud member of Lawton Alumnae Chapter of Delta Sigma Theta Sorority, Inc., where she continues to uphold the values of sisterhood, scholarship, and service in both her professional and personal life.

Her writing is an extension of her life's mission: to transform pain into purpose and empower others to find strength, healing, and hope, even in the most difficult moments.

ABOUT THE CO-AUTHOR

Amber Ward is a writer, social worker, and mental health advocate whose work is rooted in compassion, resilience, and faith. She is the Co-Founder of Even In This Enterprise, LLC. A graduate of Lawton Christian School and the University of Central Oklahoma, where she earned her Bachelor's degree in Social Work, Amber is currently pursuing her Master's degree in Social Work, continuing her commitment to serving others with empathy and excellence.

In her debut book, *Beyond the Break,* co-authored with her mother, Amber shares their deeply personal journey through grief following the loss of her beloved older brother. Drawing on her professional background and lived experience, she offers a powerful exploration of trauma, healing, and the enduring strength of human connection.

With vulnerability and grace, Amber's writing serves as both a tribute to her brother's life and a source of comfort for others navigating loss. Her voice is one of hope, reminding readers that even in the darkest seasons, healing is possible and love never fades.